Notes By Al

Notes By Al

My musical knowledge of notes was very limited. I didn't know notes and couldn't read them.

These songs are all by ear. I would write the lyrics as they came to me, put my tune to the lyrics, sing it to a cassette tape, give it to a friend of mine who would then arrange it to lead sheet or song.

Just thought these might be interesting. Some even got published.

bye

Al Vicent

Order this book online at www.trafford.com
or email orders@trafford.com

Most Trafford titles are also available at major online book retailers.

Print information available on the last page.

ISBN: 978-1-6987-1451-6 (sc)
ISBN: 978-1-6987-1450-9 (e)

Trafford rev. 04/19/2023

www.trafford.com
North America & international
toll-free: 844-688-6899 (USA & Canada)
fax: 812 355 4082

TABLE OF CONTENTS

GONNA SEE A BABY

Beacon Choral Series

Gonna See A Baby was originally published by Beacon Hill Music in 1980. It was a part of the Beacon Choral Series. The musical score was composed by Robert Brown. It was written for a flute accompaniment to be played with a joyful manner.

GONNA SEE A BABY

(S.A.T.B. with Optional Flute)

ROBERT BROWN   **AL VICENT**

*Start here in absence of flute.

We've been a look-in' for a Mar-y and Jo-seph.

Beth-a - le - hem.   Gon-na see a

Heard from an an - gel 'bout ___ a lit-tle ba - by.

ba-by born in Beth-a - le - hem.

Born in a man-ger in a Beth-a - le - hem.

1. Born in the Spir - it, born in glo -
2. Come to__ help the wea - ry soul,

- ry,

Come from the Fa - ther,
Heal the __ wound and

tell the sto - ry.
make us whole. _____

Look-in' o - ver

yon - der I   think I   see   a   bright star

Shin-in' on a sta-ble in a   Beth-a - le - hem.

Spe-cial lit-tle ba-by from a heav-en a-bove.

Why all the fuss-in' o-ver

Sent from a heav-en to a show a God's love.

just a lit-tle ba - by,

SON OF THE HIGHEST

The second time Gonna See A Baby was published was by Lillenas Publishing Co. in 1983. It was A Choral Presentation for Christmas. It was arranged by Dick Bolks with Drama by Paul M. Miller. The songbook is set up like a play with different song leading you through from the beginning to the end of the Christmas story.

GONNA SEE A BABY

ROBERT BROWN
Arr. by Dick Bolks

AL VICENT

Joyful (♩ =176)

Narrator: So it was to the shepherds that God first announced the birth of His Son. To

shepherds came word of One who would become the Good Shepherd and who would know His sheep.

9 With excitement
mf Tenor solo

Where's ev - 'ry - bod - y go -

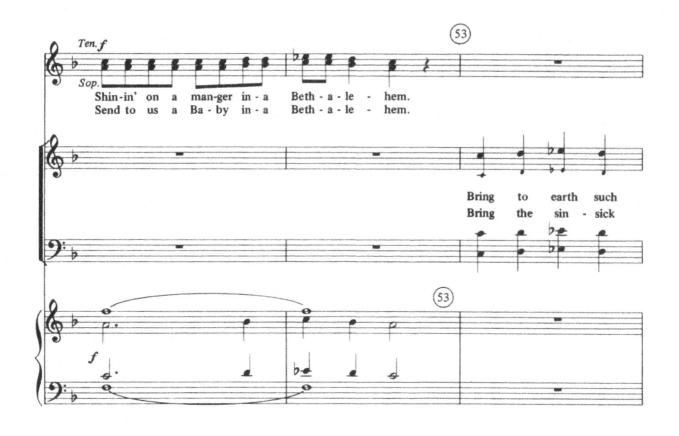

God look down from up a - bove,

Give to us a Ba - by in - a Beth - a - le - hem.

Send to us His per - fect love,

Send His Son Je - sus to show His

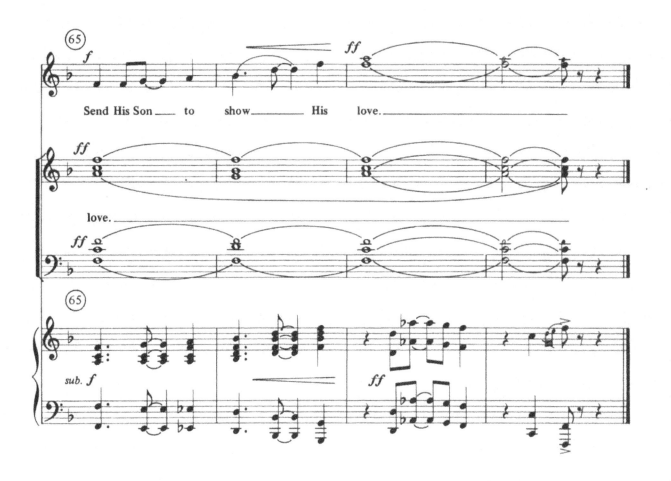

Send His Son ___ to show ___ His love. ___

love.

TABLEAU: SHEPHERDS make their way to stable and shyly enter. They kneel at the manger through following narration and song.

Narrator: And they came in haste and found their way to Mary and Joseph, and Baby Jesus as He lay in the manger.

Man 1: And those shepherds were so convinced that they had seen the Son of God . . .

Man 2: That they told everyone they met along the way.

Narrator: And all who heard the news wondered at the marvelous things they told them.

Woman: But Mary treasured all this, pondering it in her heart.

CHRISTMAS A CAPPELLA

The third time Gonna See A Baby was published was again by
Lillenas Publishing Co., this time in 2001. It was part of a
group of 23 Creative Arrangements for Choirs Large & Small.
It was arranged by Tom Fettke.

GONNA SEE A BABY

ROBERT BROWN
Arranged by Tom Fettke

AL VICENT

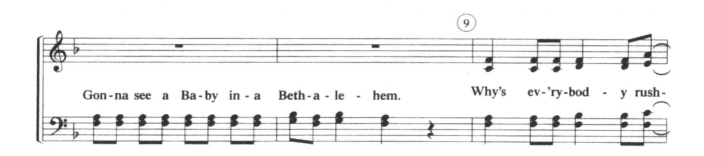

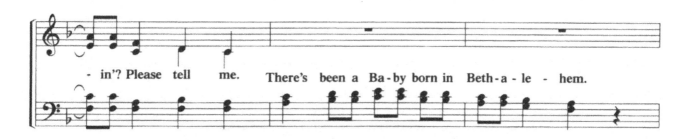

Shin-in' on a sta-ble in - a Beth - a - le - hem.
Du, du, du, Du, du, du.

Why are all the shep - herds star - - in' at the man - ger?

Look-in' at the Ba - by born in Beth - a - le - hem.
Du, du, du, Du, du, du.

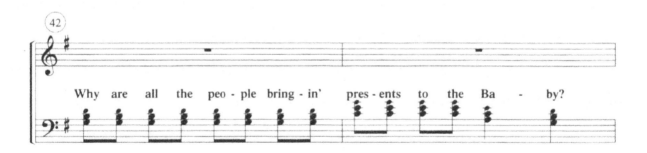

Why are all the peo - ple bring-in' pres - ents to the Ba - by?

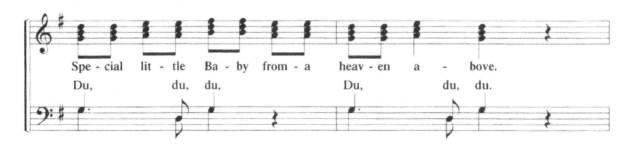

Spe - cial lit - tle Ba - by from a heav - en a - bove.
Du, du, du, Du, du, du.

THE TRAIN OF LIFE

THE TRAIN OF LIFE

Arr. by GIANNI STAIANO

AL VICENT

train would start when one was ve-ry ve-ry small   and once it would start you were then on   call This

train was on   the road of life   and each one drove from birth all through life

As a   per-son got old - er then the road got rough And the

driv-er had to watch all the curves and stuff This train was on the road of life and

each one drove from birth all through life This train had mount-ains tun-nels bridg-es to cross Kept the

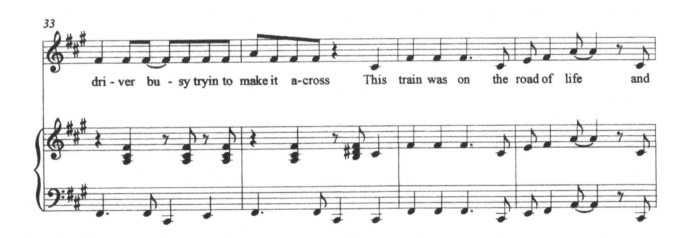

dri - ver bu - sy tryin to make it a-cross This train was on the road of life and

41

each one drove from birth all through life   there were

ma-ny temp ta - tions on the road of life   but signs were there to keep the dri-ver think-in' right This

train was   on   the road of life   and each one drove   from birth all through life

God and his an - gels were at___ the last stop each train tried hard to get___ to this stop This

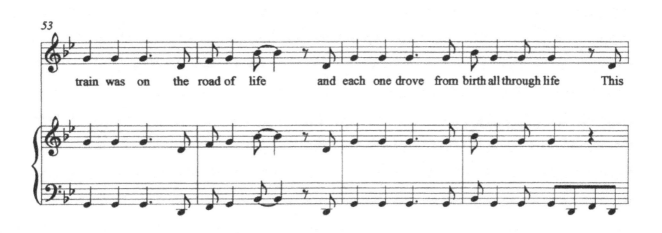

train was on the road of life and each one drove from birth all through life This

train it was a run-nin in a vis-ion in the night This train it was a run-nin in a vis-ion in the night a

run-nin a run-nin a run-nin a run-nin This train was a run-nin in the night This

train was a run-nin in the night

rall.

EXCUSE ME

EXCUSE ME

AL VICENT

Ex-cuse me please but did you hap-pen to see Je - sus For I was told that he might pass this way to - day That he might stop share his

bless-ings and min-gle with us   Ex-cuse me please but did you

see him   pass this way to-day?   oh if he

passed   did he leave   a mes-sage   Was there a

sign that he might pass this way a - gain Did he

stop heal the sick and help the low - ly? Ex-cuse me

please but did you see Je sus___ pass this way to- day?

None passed this way ex cept the stran-ger who said, Come let the lit-tle

chil-dren sit on my knee. But they said the stran ger's arms were open

wide and from somewhere deep down in - side That love just flowed and in it's

più mosso

meno mosso

THE WAYS OF GOD

THE WAYS OF GOD

AL VICENT

THERE'S A REASON

THERE'S A REASON

Arr. by GIANNI STAIANO

AL VICENT

A FLAG

A FLAG

AL VICENT

SALINAS

SALINAS

Cowboy Waltz

AL VICENT

The ci-ty___ of Sa - li - nas,___ Ca - li - for - nia
Ro - de - o's___ in the ci - ty___ bring the crowds out

ram - bling___ through the val leys___ near the hills   has a
they're classed as the ve - ry best in the land   and the

beau - ty that will charm you   for - ev - er___   takes of
warm balm - y___ days in   the val - ley___   makes the

love and wants you for its'___ ve - ry own.   Oh my
wea - ther ve - ry love-ly___ and___ grand.   Oh you

heart will___ al - ways be in___ Sa - li - nas   For friends are
can lose___ your true heart in___ Sa - li - nas   in the

there I'm wel - come a - ny___ time   Her op - en
peace - ful hap - py living of the town   or just

skies and green fields seem to call me___ ev - er
soft moon filled nights in the val- ley___ might make

si - lent ev - er love- ly___ in my mind Sa-
you want to___ stay in___ that___ town

li - nas___ Sa - li - nas___ Sa - li - nas___ Oh you

call out so clear- ly to me Sa -

li - nas___ Sa - li - nas___ Sa - li - nas___ A

ci - ty___ in the Gold - en val- ley___

RUTH

RUTH

Gospel Swing

AL VICENT

A SONG CAN GO ANYWHERE

A SONG CAN GO ANYWHERE

AL VICENT

THIS THANKSGIVING DAY

THIS THANKSGIVING DAY

AL VICENT

CHRISTMAS TIME

CHRISTMAS TIME

AL VICENT

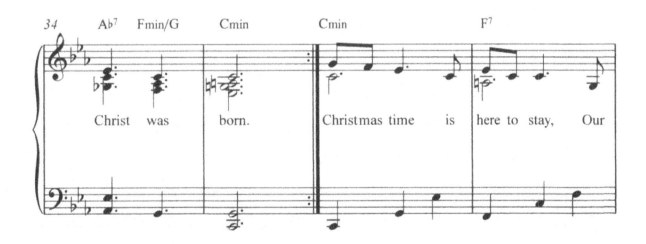

sav-ior's birth is here to day, Can't you feel the Christmas cheer?

Christ is born, Christmas is here. Christmas time,

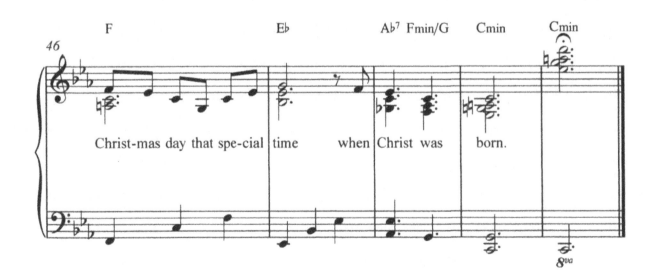

Christ-mas day that spe-cial time when Christ was born.

PRAY TO GOD

PRAY TO GOD

AL VICENT

Pray to
strength to

God from where you are, He will
all who pray, Gives them

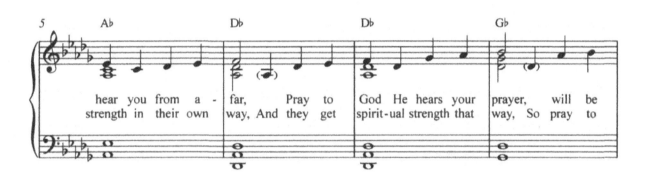

hear you from a -
strength in their own

far, Pray to
way, And they get

God He hears your
spirit-ual strength that

prayer, will be
way, So pray to

with you and He'll
God some-where to -

care. Pray to
day. God hears

God in your own
prayers of those who

way, Be sure you
pray, and bless - es

2

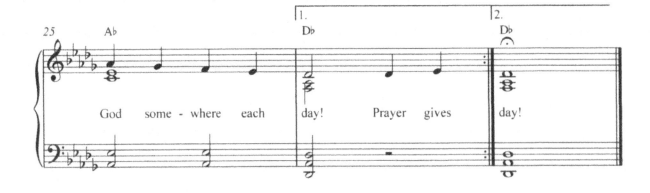

THE CRUCIFIXION

ARRANGED BY GIANNI STAIANO

The following is a finalized version of the crucifixion. It is arranged by Gianni Staiano. It will shown in comparison to Al's originally written version and will demonstrate the way the music can change a small amount from the original to the finalized version.

THE CRUCIFIXION

Arranged by Gianni Staiano

AL VICENT

he'll re - turn____ oh he'll come back a - gain____

ORIGINAL VERSION

This version of the crucifixion is how it was originally written by Al. From this point on all the song will be the orginal versions by Al.

THE CRUCIFIXION

THE SPIRIT OF GOD

THE SPIRIT OF GOD

THE SPIRIT OF GOD

WORDS AND MUSIC BY
AL VICENT

DRIV-IN' OUT HATE...THE SPIR-IT OF GOD...IT'S A MOV-IN' IN THE LAND. THE
FAM-I-LIES TO-GETH-ER...THE SPIR-IT OF GOD... IT'S A MOV-IN' IN THE LAND. THE

D.S. ½. AL CODA

CODA

(5,6.) SPIR-IT OF GOD...IT'S A MOV-IN' AND A RUMB-LIN'...THE SPIR-IT OF GOD...IT'S A

MOV-IN' IN THE LAND. THE SPIR-IT OF GOD...IS___ NEED-ED BY THE NAT-IONS...THE
THE SPIR-IT OF GOD GIVES LOV-IN' WORLD PEACE____...THE

SPIR-IT OF GOD...IT'S A MOV-IN' IN THE LAND. THE
SPIR-IT OF GOD...IT'S A MOV-IN' IN THE LAND. THE

D.S. ½. AL FINE

LET YOUR LIGHT SHINE

LET YOUR LIGHT SHINE

LET YOUR LIGHT SHINE

SPIR·IT __ IS THE CAN·DLE FROM GOD __ — MAN'S SPIR __ IT __ IS __ THE

CANDLE FROM GOD BRIGH·TEN YOUR DAY __ LET YOUR LIGHT SHINE __ BRIGH·TEN THE

DAY __ LET YOUR LIGHT SHINE __ .

GOD GIVES

LIGHT __ OUT OF THE DARK __ GOD GIVES LIGHT __ OUT OF THE DARK LET GOD'S SPIR

SHINE __ BRIGH·TEN THE DAY __ LET GOD'S SPIR·IT SHINE __ BRIGH·TEN YOUR

WAY __ WALK IN THE

GO, TELL THE PEOPLE

GO, TELL THE PEOPLE

WORDS AND MUSIC BY
AL VICENT

GOD A-BOVE ___ THE CHILD IS THE SAV-IOR SENT FROM GOD A-BOVE ___.

GO, TELL THE PEO-PLE ALL THE AN-GELS ARE SING ___ ING ___, TELL ALL THE PEO-PLE ALL THE

AN-GELS ARE SING ___ ING ___, GO, TELL THE PEO-PLE ALL THE SHEP-HERDS ARE COM ___ ING ___,

TELL ALL THE PEO-PLE THE SHEP-HERDS ARE COM ___ ING ... TELL ALL ___ THE PEO ___

___ PLE ___ .

ROLL ON, CHARIOT

ROLL ON, CHARIOT

122

SOME SWEET DAY

SOME SWEET DAY
Some Sweet Day

WORDS AND MUSIC BY
AL VICENT

DAY ___ WHEN HE CALLS... SOME SWEET DAY. PRAY ON . PRAY AND BE

REA_DY.. JE _ SUS WILL COME.. YOU BE REA_DY... SOME SWEET

DAY _ , SOME SWEET DAY _____ WHEN HE CALLS ___ SOME SWEET DAY. WE'LL

D.S. AL
fine

LOVE

WAITIN'
(FOR SALINAS TRAIN)

WAITIN'
(FOR SALINAS TRAIN)

I'm waitin' for
The Train
I'm waintin' for
The Train
I'm waitin' for
The Train to Salinas

Oh where– oh where
Oh where– oh where
Oh where in the world
Is Salinas

It's way out West
Where the Broccoli grows

It's way out west
Where there's Cowboys too

It's way out west
That's the place for you

Way out West
In Salinas

What will you do
When you get out there

What will you do in Salinas

I'll pretend I'm a cowboy
When I get out there

Ride and old grey horse
That's and an old grey mare

That's what I'll do
I'll do, I'll do
That's what I'll do
When I get to Salinas.

Waitin'

Albert Vicent

133